It's all about...

SPECTACULAR SHIPS

KINGFISHER

KINGFISHER

First published 2016 by Kingfisher
an imprint of Macmillan Children's Books
20 New Wharf Road, London N1 9RR
Associated companies throughout the world
www.panmacmillan.com

Series editor: Sarah Snashall
Series design: Anthony Hannant (LittleRedAnt)
Written by Sarah Snashall

ISBN 978-0-7534-3942-5

9 8 7 6 5 4 3 2 1

1TR/1115/WKT/UG/128MA

A CIP catalogue record for this book is available from the British Library.

Printed in China

Picture credits
The Publisher would like to thank the following for permission to reproduce their material.
Top = t; Bottom = b; Centre = c; Left = l; Right = r
Cover Shutterstock/E.G.Pors; Back cover Shutterstock/Jeanette Dieti; Page 1 Shutterstock/E.G.Pors; 2–3, 16–17, 30–31 Shutterstock/bcampbell65; 4 Shutterstock/Silia Photo; 5 Shutterstock/OzPhotoguy; 6–7 Shutterstock/Ronnie Chua; 7 Alamy/Ancient Art & Architecture Collection; 8 Alamy/Pictorial Press; 8–9 Shutterstock/Joseph Sohm; 10 Shutterstock/Patryk Kosmider; 11 Shutterstock/Everett Historical; 12 Bridgeman/National Geographic Creative/Robert McGinnes; 13t Getty/Peter Ptschelinzew; 13b Getty/Hulton Archive/Stringer; 14 Alamy/World History Archive; 15 Alamy/Chris Hellier; 15t Picture Desk/Chris Deakes; 17t Shutterstock/Victor Maschek; 17b Alamy/imageBROKER; 18–19 Getty/Photo12; 19t Getty/Scott Polar Research Institute, University of Cambrige; 20–21 Alamy/nidpor; 21t Corbis/Ralph White; 22–23 Photobucket; 23t, 25 MoD Crown; 24 koreaonthego; 26 Kyle D Gahlau; 27 victor-ny; 27t US Navy/Zack Baddorf; 28 Alamy/aerial-photos.com; 29t Juliet Marine Systems.
Cards: Front tl Flickr/John Chouvardas; tr Shutterstock/Joseph Sohm; bl Shutterstock/Colin Hutchings; Back tl Shutterstock/Altormmfoto; tr Alamy/GL Archive; bl Flickr/US Navy; br Flickr/Kees torn.

Front cover: A fully loaded container ship leaves port with the help of a tugboat.

CONTENTS

For your free audio download go to
http://panmacmillan.com/SpectacularShips
or goo.gl/S6e26z
Happy listening!

From log to liner	4
Early traders	6
Voyages of discovery	8
Beware of pirates!	10
Life on board	12
Leaving home	14
Shipwreck!	16
An icy adventure	18
Titanic	20
Hard work	22
Ships at war	24
Above and below	26
Ships of the future	28
Glossary	30
Index	32

From log to liner

Long ago people built boats by hollowing out logs or weaving plant rushes together. Since those early days, we have built bigger boats and better ships: ships for transporting goods, ships for trading, ships for invading and ships for adventure.

Vikings travelled in their longships from Scandinavia to Africa, Greenland and Canada.

SPOTLIGHT: Allure of the Sea

Famous for: world's largest passenger ship
Height: 362 m
Capacity: 6296 passengers and 2000+ crew
Maiden voyage: 1 December, 2010

Enormous cruise liners carry thousands of passengers. They are like floating towns.

FACT...

Viking chiefs and nobles were buried in ships filled with luxury goods.

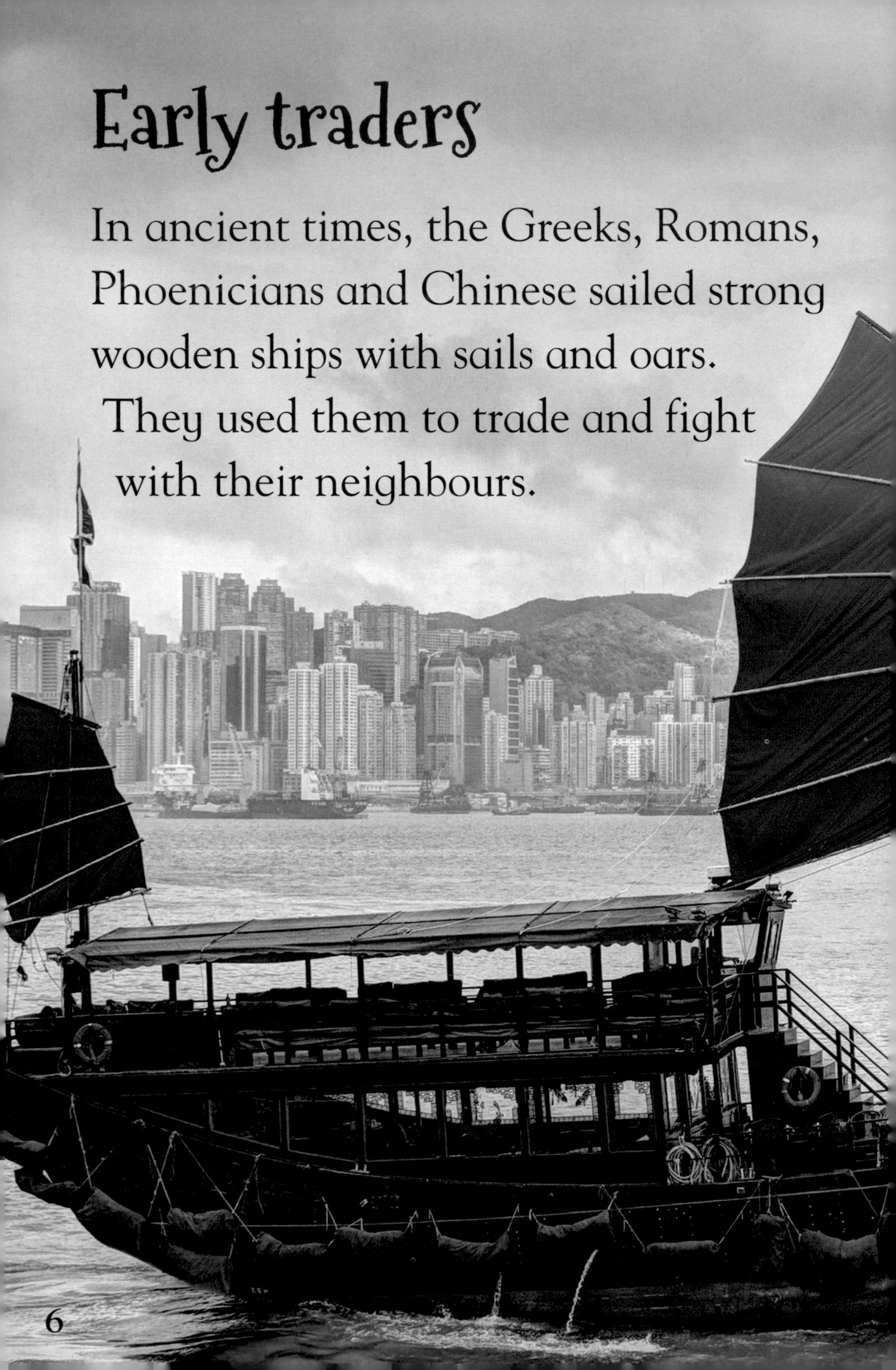

Early traders

In ancient times, the Greeks, Romans, Phoenicians and Chinese sailed strong wooden ships with sails and oars. They used them to trade and fight with their neighbours.

FACT...

Chinese junks had rudders and compasses 1000 years before ships in Europe did.

Triremes were fast warships used by the ancient Greeks and Romans. They had sails and up to 170 oarsmen who rowed for six hours a day.

Chinese junks, similar to those used by the ancient Chinese, are still in use today.

Voyages of discovery

As ships became stronger and could travel further, adventurers went on voyages of discovery to look for exotic spices, new lands and fame. Their ships had large square sails to catch the wind and cross the oceans faster. There was room on board for about 80 men and 20 cannons.

The English explorer Francis Drake sailed the *Golden Hind* around the world.

FACT...

When the explorer Christopher Columbus arrived in the Americas on 12 October, 1492, he thought he had arrived in the East Indies.

This ship is a replica of the *Santa Maria*, in which Christopher Columbus first sailed to the Americas.

Beware of pirates!

By the 1600s, the seas were full of large galleons carrying gold from the Americas and spices from the East Indies. These were rich pickings for pirates! Pirates would attack ships, steal their goods and often kill the sailors.

Spanish galleons were powerful ships with five masts.

Pirates flew the Jolly Roger, or a plain black flag, to frighten the other ships.

FACT...

Pirates often shared the treasure fairly among themselves and voted on who should be captain.

The pirate Blackbeard sailed a ship called the *Queen Anne's Revenge*. It carried 40 cannons.

Life on board

Do you fancy a life at sea? If you ran away to sea 400 years ago, you might regret it quite soon. You would sleep wherever you could find space. Food would be salted meat and dry biscuits – perhaps filled with weevils! You would be at sea for months without washing or changing your clothes.

Without fresh food to eat, people were in danger of catching a disease called scurvy.

FACT...

Spanish sailors visiting the West Indies saw locals sleeping in hammocks. Soon sailors started using them on board ships.

Each ship had a surgeon who cut hair and amputated diseased limbs.

Leaving home

In 1620, 102 'pilgrims' left Plymouth, England on a merchant ship called the *Mayflower* to start a new life in America. Since then, many thousands have travelled on ships to start new lives abroad. From 1820 to 1920, 18 million people sailed from Europe to settle in America.

Pilgrims board the *Mayflower* in Plymouth, England.

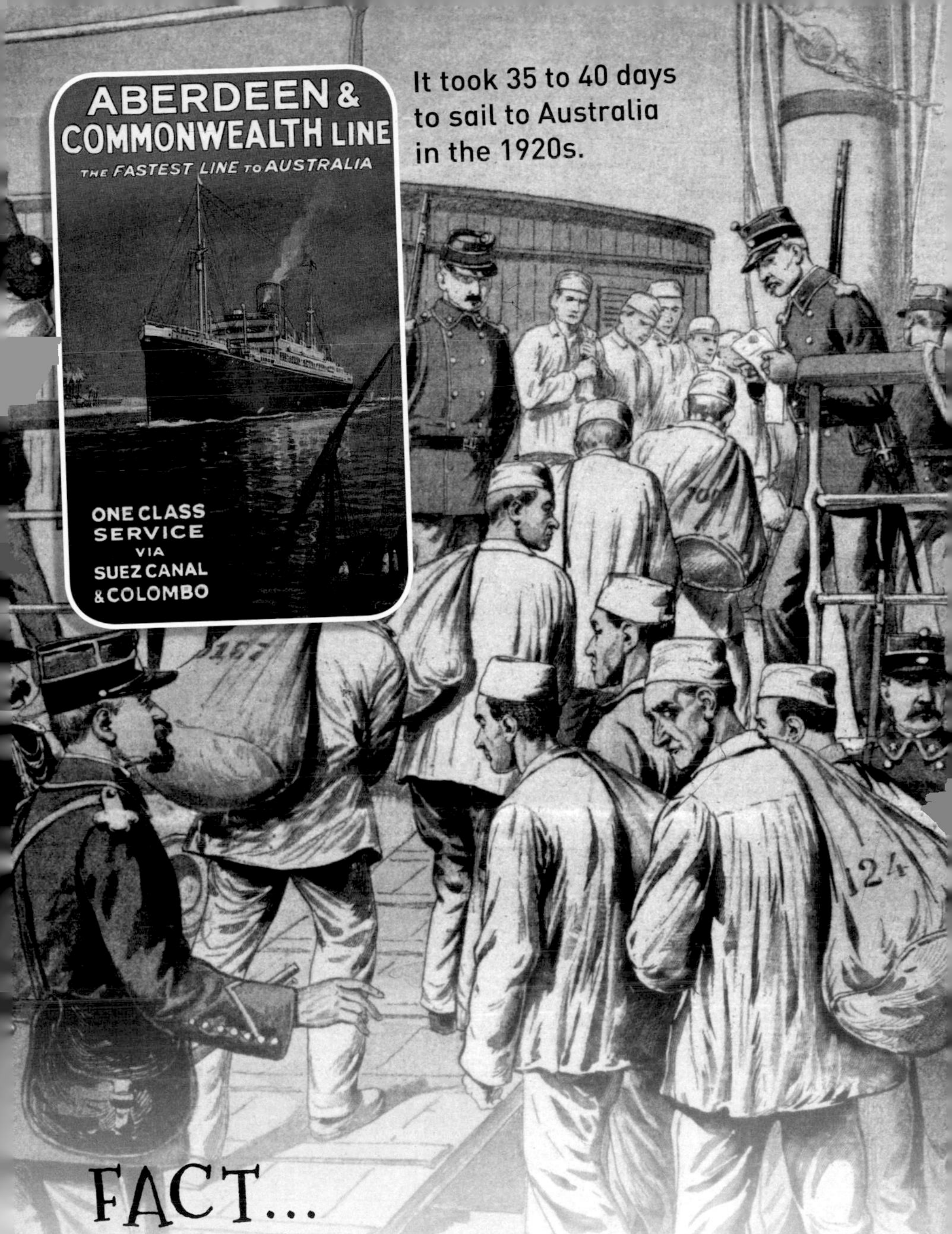

It took 35 to 40 days to sail to Australia in the 1920s.

FACT...

For two hundred years, the British Government sent prisoners to prison villages in America and then Australia. Most people chose to stay there.

Shipwreck!

The sea is a dangerous place. Over the centuries, ships have been sunk by whales, waves and rocks. Most ships were broken up by the sea but some sank into the mud, waiting to be discovered by divers.

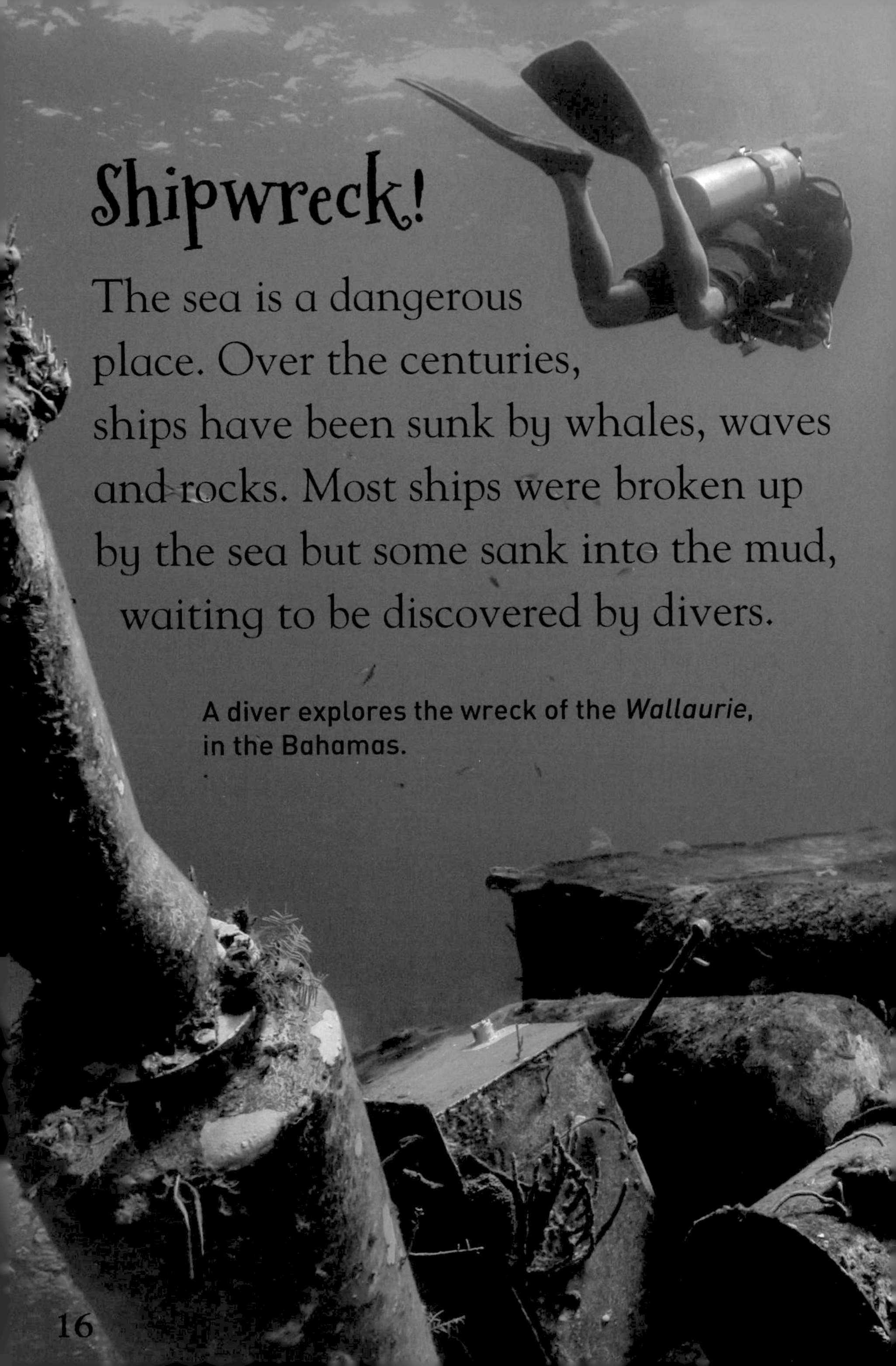

A diver explores the wreck of the *Wallaurie*, in the Bahamas.

The Swedish ship the *Vasa* sank in 1628 on its first voyage. In 1961 it was brought to the surface.

Shipwrecks can tell us about life on board the ship.

An icy adventure

Fridtjof Nansen designed a very strong boat for his unsuccessful attempt to sail to the North Pole. The *Fram* was trapped in the ice for three years but the crew were comfortable: the *Fram* had an insulated hull, an electric generator, plenty of food and a piano.

The *Fram* had three masts and an engine. It was shallow and wide to withstand the ice.

Ernest Shackleton's ship the *Endurance* was trapped for 10 months before it was crushed by the ice.

SPOTLIGHT: Fram

Famous for:	polar expedition ship
Height:	38.9 m
Capacity:	16 men
Maiden voyage:	1893

FACT...

The Norwegian explorer Roald Amundsen used the *Fram* when he went to the South Pole.

Titanic

The luxury passenger liner *Titanic* left Southampton for New York on 10 April, 1912. It had many magnificent rooms but it did not have enough lifeboats. On 14 April, the *Titanic* hit an iceberg and sank. A total of 1500 people lost their lives.

The *Titanic* had two huge steam engines and could travel at 44 km/h.

SPOTLIGHT: Titanic

Famous for:	hitting an iceberg
Height:	269 m
Capacity:	2435 passengers plus 892 crew
Maiden voyage:	1893

FACT...

Many of the *Titanic's* lifeboats were launched half full, and only 710 people were saved.

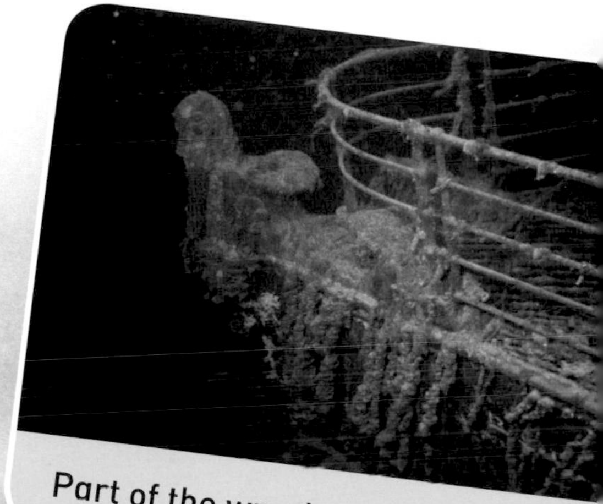

Part of the wreck of the *Titanic*.

Hard work

Today, the oceans are filled with hard-working ships. Thousands of huge cargo ships cross the world's shipping lanes carrying goods and oil. There are also ice breakers, fishing trawlers, research ships and ships that lay internet cables on the seabed.

FACT...

Supertanker *Knock Nevis* was longer than the height of the Empire State Building in New York.

Ice breakers are strong enough to break through ice. The ship's hull is shaped to push the ice out of the way.

SPOTLIGHT: Knock Nevis

Famous for:	longest and heaviest ship
Height:	458 m
Capacity:	564,763 tonnes of oil
Maiden voyage:	1979

Ships at war

The toughest ships have always been warships. These ships have the biggest guns, the fastest speeds and the strongest hulls. Early warships were built of thick oak and armed with cannons. Today, warships have iron hulls and big guns and torpedoes.

The Korean turtle ship was armed with a sulphur gas thrower, iron spikes and cannons.

Spotlight: HMS Victory

Famous for:	Battle of Trafalgar
Height:	69 m
Capacity:	about 850 sailors and soldiers
Maiden voyage:	1765

HMS Victory, the flagship of Britain's Admiral Nelson, had 104 cannons.

HMS Argyll is a very fast-moving warship. The ship patrols the Caribbean looking for drug smugglers.

Above and below

In modern wars, destroyers can launch missiles at a target hundreds of kilometres away. Fighter planes, surveillance planes and helicopters can take off and land on aircraft carriers. Under the sea, submarines spy on enemy ships.

About 3000 people live and work on board an aircraft carrier.

A nuclear submarine can stay underwater until the food runs out.

FACT...

USS Triton was the first submarine to travel around the world underwater.

SPOTLIGHT: USS Nautilus

Famous for:	first nuclear submarine
Height:	98 m
Capacity:	105 submariners
Maiden voyage:	1954

Ships of the future

What will ships look like in the future? Some will be bigger, some will be faster and others will save fuel by using solar panels and sails, or by floating on a cushion of gas or bubbles.

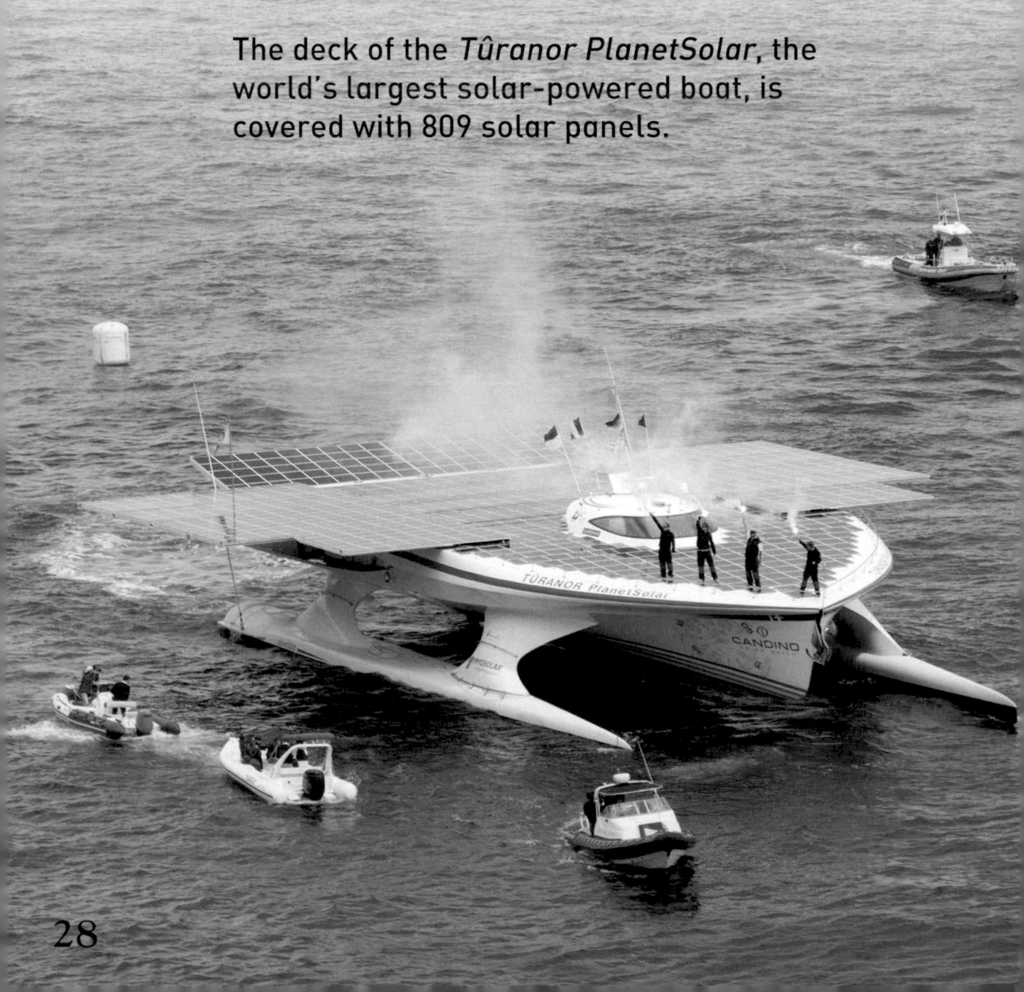

The deck of the *Tûranor PlanetSolar*, the world's largest solar-powered boat, is covered with 809 solar panels.

Is it a boat? Is it a plane? The *GHOST* marine platform is a stealth ship that moves on gas bubbles to travel faster.

FACT...

The *GHOST* marine platform has been designed to attack modern-day pirates.

The hull of this Swedish stealth ship the *Helsingborg* is made of carbon fibre and vinyl to make it difficult to detect.

GLOSSARY

aircraft carrier A warship with a large flat area from which small aircraft take off and land.

cargo ship A ship designed to carry goods.

compass An instrument that points to north and can be used to navigate.

cruise liner A large ship for holidaymakers which travels from port to port.

destroyer A small heavily armed ship that protects larger warships.

galleon A large sailing ship with square sails used for war and trade.

hull The main body of the ship (not including the masts).

mast A tall upright post that carries the sails.

nuclear submarine An underwater vessel that is powered by a nuclear reactor.

pirate A robber who attacks ships from another ship or boat.

rigging A system of ropes that support a ship's mast and operate the sails.

rudder A movable flat piece of wood or metal that sticks out from the bottom and back of a ship and is used to steer it.

solar panel A flat plate that converts energy from the sun into another form of energy such as electricity.

spice A food flavouring grown in hot parts of the world.

supertanker An enormous oil tanker.

surveillance Watching something closely, often without being seen.

tanker A ship that carries large amounts of oil.

torpedo An underwater missile.

trireme An ancient Greek or Roman ship with three rows of oars.

INDEX

aircraft carriers 26
Allure of the Sea 5
America 9, 10, 14, 15
Amundsen, Roald 19
Australia 15

cargo ships 22
Chinese, ancient 6, 7
Columbus, Christopher 9
cruise liners 5

destroyers 26
Drake, Francis 8

Egyptians, ancient 7

fishing trawlers 22
Fram 18–19

galleons 10
Golden Hind 8
Greeks, ancient 6, 7

HMS Victory 25
hulls 18, 24, 29

ice breakers 22, 23
invasion 4

Knock Nevis 22–23

life on board 12–13, 17

Mayflower 14

Nansen, Fridtjof 18
nuclear submarines 27

oil tankers 22

Phoenicians, ancient 6
pirates 10–11, 29

Romans, ancient 6, 7

Santa Maria 9
Shackleton, Ernest 19
shipwrecks 16–17
spices 8, 10
supertankers 22–23

torpedoes 24
trade 6
transport 4
triremes 6, 7
turtle ship 24

Vasa 17
Vikings 4–5

SPECTACULAR SHIPS
Collector Card

SPECTACULAR SHIPS
Collector Card

SPECTACULAR SHIPS
Collector Card

SPECTACULAR SHIPS
Collector Card

Allure of the Sea

The largest cruise ship in the world has 24 lifts.

	SCORE
LENGTH: 362 m	9
PEOPLE ON BOARD: 8296	10
TOP SPEED: 42 km/h	8
DEADLINESS:	0

Bismarck

The famous German battleship from World War II.

	SCORE
LENGTH: 251 m	6
PEOPLE ON BOARD: 2065	7
TOP SPEED: 56 km/h	10
DEADLINESS: 62 huge guns	8

USS Nimitz aircraft carrier

A huge nuclear-powered aircraft carrier that can hold 90 aircraft.

	SCORE
LENGTH: 332 m	8
PEOPLE ON BOARD: 5680	9
TOP SPEED: 56 km/h	10
DEADLINESS: 90 fighter jets	10

MSC Oscar

The largest container ship in the world can carry 19,224 containers.

	SCORE
LENGTH: 396 m	10
PEOPLE ON BOARD: 35	1
TOP SPEED: 42 km/h	8
DEADLINESS:	0

Collect all the titles in this series!